GEORGE BENJAMIN

SHADOWLINES

six canonic preludes for piano

(2001)

FABER **ff** MUSIC

The first performance was given by Pierre-Laurent Aimard in the Barbican Hall, London,
as part of the London Symphony Orchestra's *By George!* Festival
on 13 February 2003

Duration: *c.*15 minutes

Shadowlines is recorded by Pierre-Laurent Aimard
on Nimbus Records NI 5713 (CD)

Performance Note
Accidentals apply throughout the bar

To buy Faber Music publications or to find out about the full range of titles available
please contact your local music retailer or Faber Music sales enquiries:

Faber Music Limited, Burnt Mill, Elizabeth Way, Harlow, CM20 2HX England
Tel: +44 (0)1279 82 89 82   Fax: +44 (0)1279 82 89 83
sales@fabermusic.com   fabermusic.com

PROGRAMME NOTE

This sequence of pieces, all canons in different ways, was conceived as a continuous, cumulative structure:

I   A brief, seemingly improvisatory prologue.

II   The higher register, fierce and harshly chromatic, against the lower, which is consonant and calm; a compact coda reconciles these opposites.

III A miniature scherzo, all within the space of 1½ octaves in the bass, leading immediately to:

IV   Explosive and monolithic, the pianist's hands perpetually rifting apart then re-uniting in rhythmical unison.

V   The most expansive and lyrical movement; at its heart a slow ground bass, over which builds a widely contrasted procession of textures. After a short pause:

VI   A gentle, flowing epilogue.

This work was written for Pierre-Laurent Aimard, and was commissioned by Betty Freeman.

GB

Happily commissioned by Betty Freeman

SHADOWLINES

for Pierre-Laurent

I

GEORGE BENJAMIN

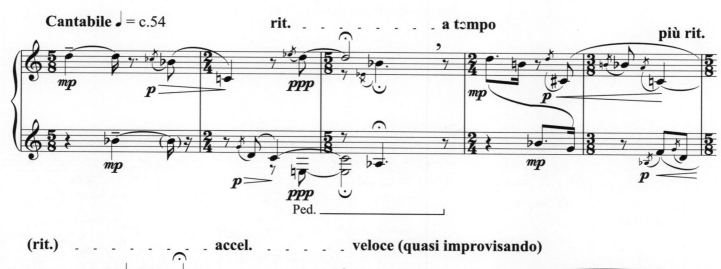

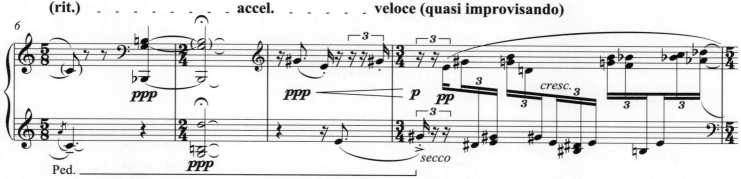

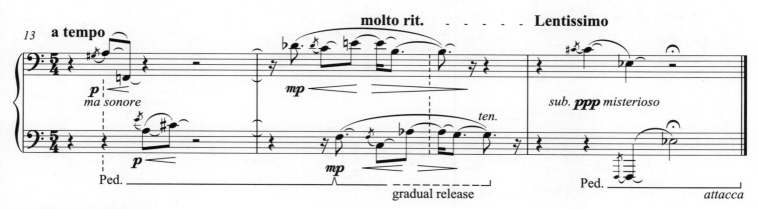

2

for Pierre-Laurent

II

Wild ♪. = 144

marcatissimo, feroce

ff sempre

(silent)

tranquillo, legatissimo
non espressivo

Ped. III (until bar 34)

pppp sempre

ff

5

pppp sub.

sff

sub. ff marcatiss.

sff

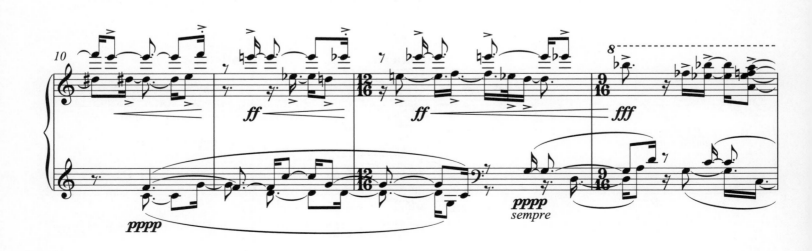

10

ff

ff

fff

pppp

pppp
sempre

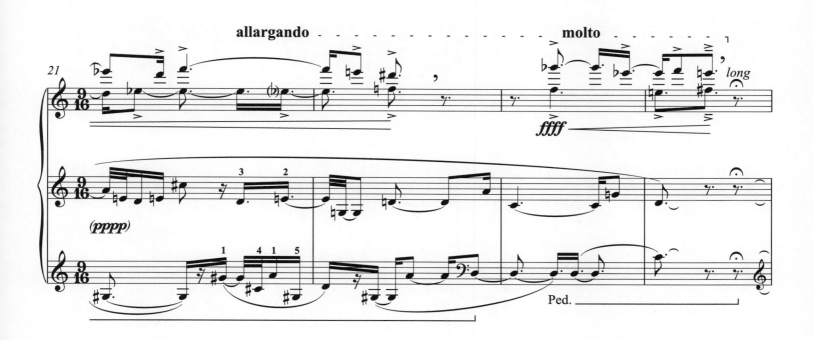

4

a tempo ma molto tranquillo

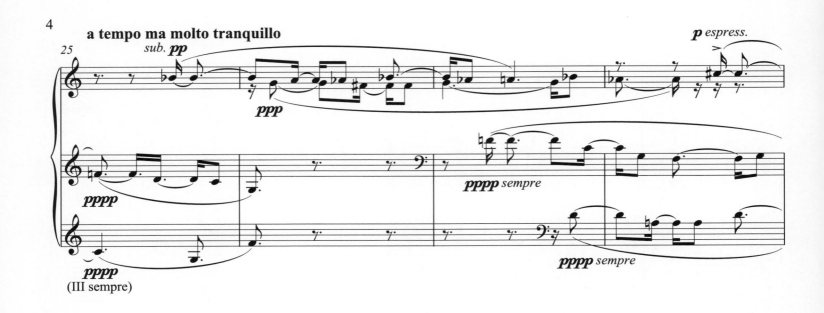

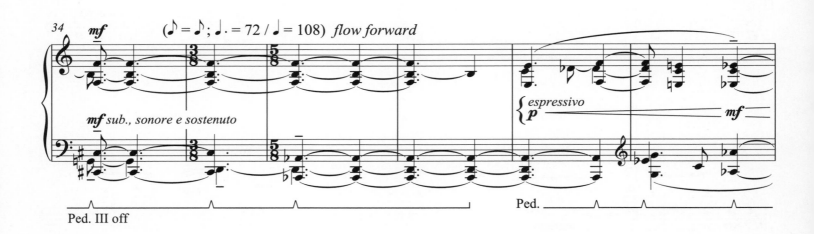

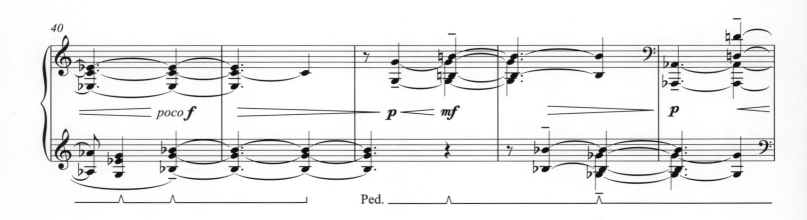

poco

attacca

for Pierre-Laurent

III

Scherzando ♩. = c.84

8

for Betty on her 80th birthday

IV

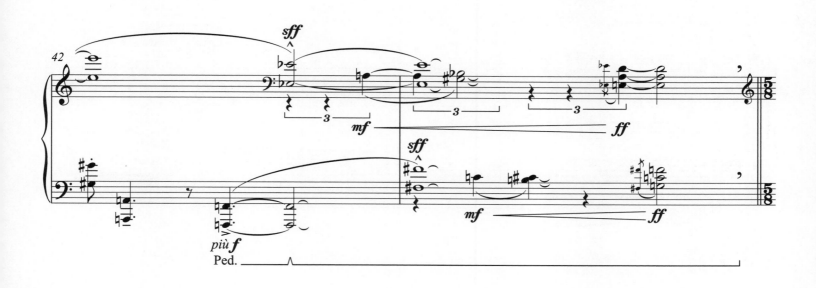

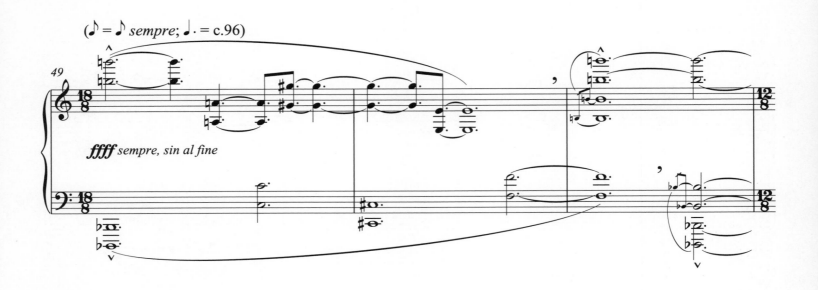

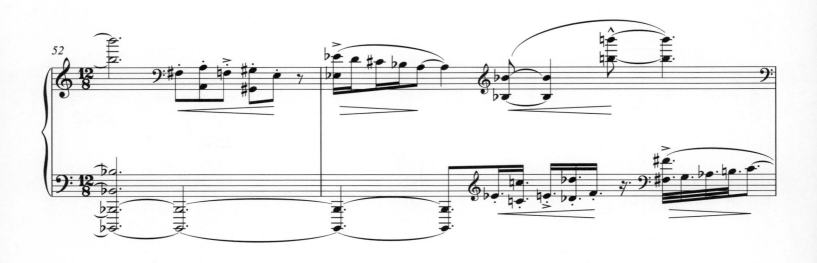

long pause
before movement V

for Olly on his 50th birthday

V

Spacious and solemn ♪ = 72

pp ma sonore

III

(III)

(III)

III

Ped. _____   Ped. _____

III

Ped. _____

sim.

pp secco

Ped. _____

mp dolcissimo

* bass line: *pp*, even and regular, at all times

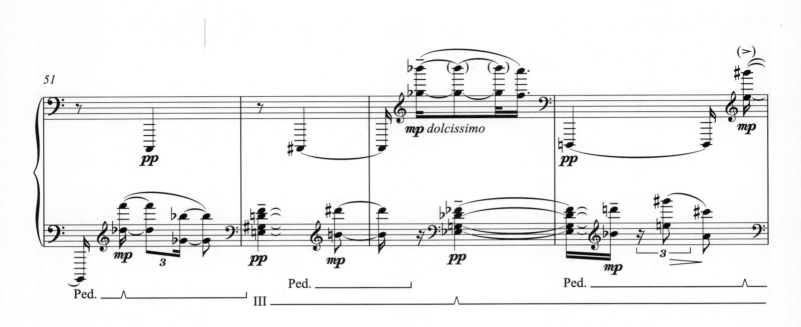

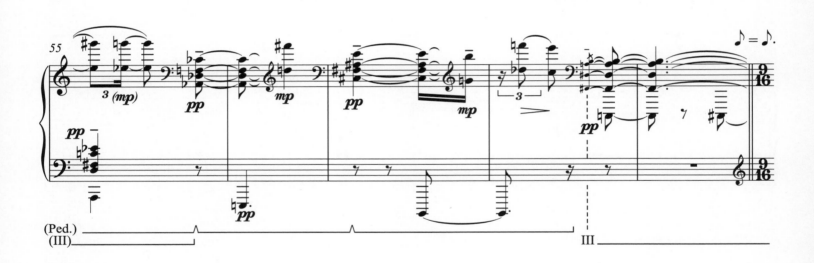

Imperceptibly faster (♩. = 80)

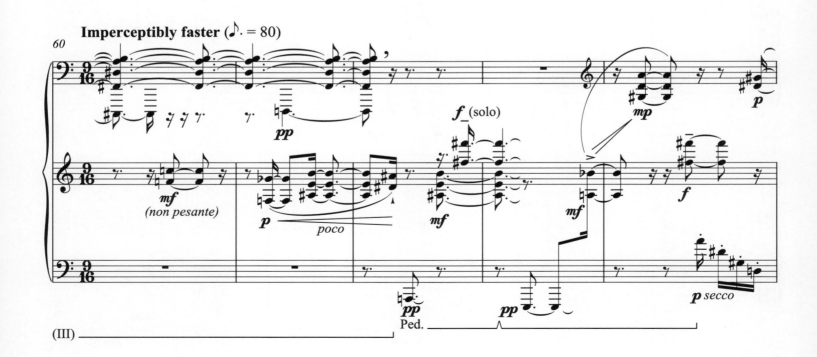

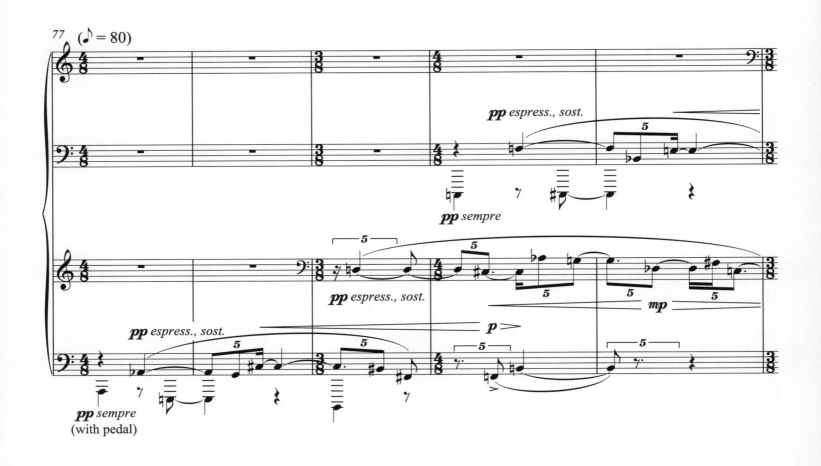

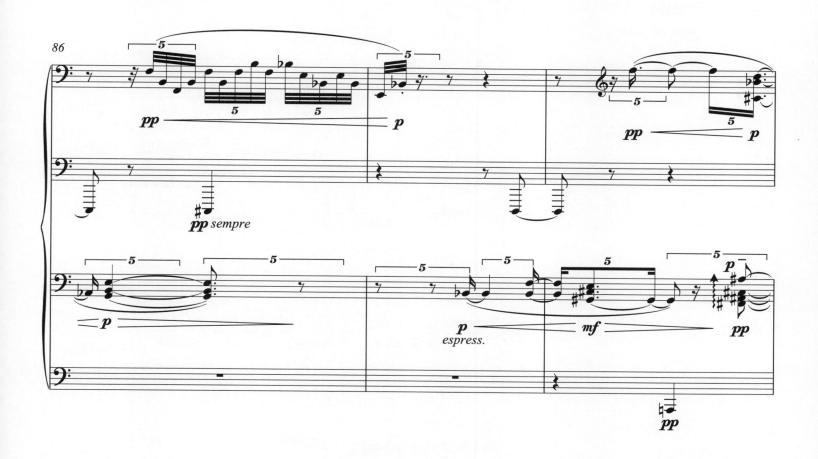

for B. and S. on their 50th

VI

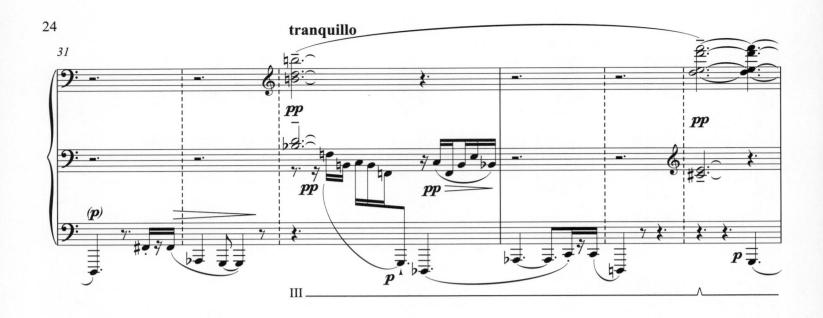

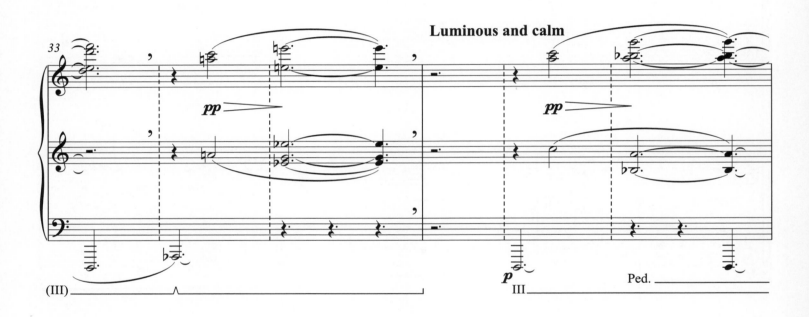

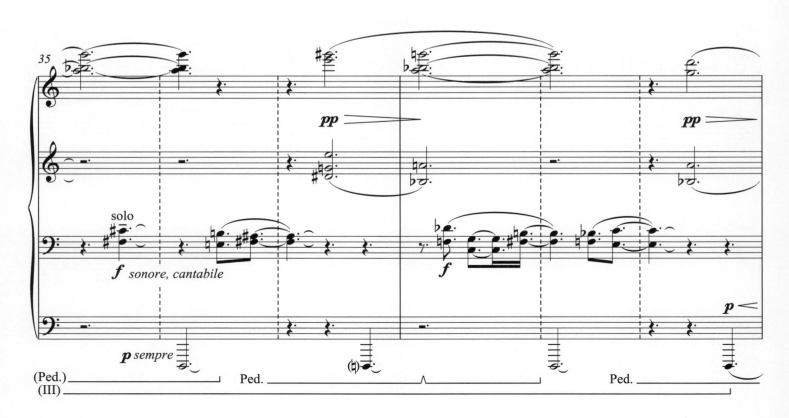